The Code of Patrick Süskind's Perfume

Truth and fiction in the text of the famous novel

Saint Petersburg, 2017

UDC 94(4)

LBC 63.3(0)51

B82

Borzenko, Semyon Borisovich.

B82   The Code of Patrick Süskind's Perfume
Truth and fiction in the text of the famous novel - SPb: Zhivaya is-
toria, 2017.

ISBN: 978-5-9908281-2-4

Author's Note.

Patrick Süskind's "Perfume" is without a co-opinion, a literary sensation of the late 20th century. A copy of the novel can be found in the hands of a secretary in the door of the subway car and resting under the Spanish sun from the just and unjust deeds of the boss of hers, a business shark. You actually know that yourself. Much of the contents of the novel raises a number of an attentive reader's questions, in particular, about the mores and lives of the Europeans in that times, about perfumery and prototypes of the main character, about the possibility of creating a universal flavor of love, etc. Let us try to figure it out...

CHAPTER I.

Did Jean-Baptiste Grenouille Have A Real Prototype?

In eighteenth-century France there lived a man who was one of the most gifted and abominable personages in an era that knew no lack of gifted and abominable personages. His story will be told here. His name was Jean-Baptiste Grenouille, and if his name—in contrast to the names of other gifted abominations, de Sade's, for instance, or Saint-Just's, Fouché's, Bonaparte's, etc.—has been forgotten today, it is certainly not because Grenouille fell short of those more famous black-guards when it came to arrogance, misanthropy, immorality, or, more succinctly, to wickedness, but because his gifts and his sole ambition were restricted to a domain that leaves no traces in history: to the fleet-ing realm of scent.

Patrick Süskind.
"Perfume: The Story of a Murderer"

Admittedly, **Perfume: The Story of a Murderer** is by no means pure fiction. The creators of flavors in pursuit of income and fame did not breeze even the most disgusting means. at the view of the modern humanist. A Sorbonne professor, perfumery historian Annick Le Guerer cites a remarkable recipe compiled by alchem-ist and medic Oswald Croll (Crollius) (1560-1608).

not sure what this process was supposed to do

Mummies and "fresh meat"

According to Crollius, the effect of favors entering the precious mummy can be enhanced many times at the expense of an ingre-dient that is as close to life as possible. Namely, the body of a

5

young man who died by violent death. The pharmacist perfume was recommended to acquire the corpse of the just executed offender, preferably by hanging, wheeling or planting on a stake, young (ideally for some reason 24-year-old) and, preferably, red-haired, because red color is a sign of life force. Then it was necessary to separate the meat parts, sink the fat, wash well with wine alcohol and keep under solar and moon rays two days and two nights to clean the "life principles" contained in the flesh. Then rub them with myrrh, saffron and aloe and finally hang over the fire, "as they do with bull tongues and gammon of bacon that suspend over the hearth so they acquire a delightful fragrance."

The torturers earned well by selling to pharmacists parts
of the bodies of the executed criminals.

The time span from the moment of creation of the recipe to the time of action of Süskind's novel embraced only a century and a half. Quite a small period of time.

The recipe was not banned, on the contrary, it was well known to specialists. Crollius was not sent to the gallows for his monstrous recommendations; moreover, he served as court lecturer of the Holy Roman Emperor Rudolf II. It is safe to assume that both the author himself and many perfumers familiar with his statements experimented with human flesh in pursuit of profit and fame. The executed criminals of Crollius are not Grenouille's young virgins, but we are now interested in the idea of using human corpses for perfumery and medical purposes.

It started in medieval Egypt. I. P. Neymivakin in his book "Salajeet. Myths and Reality" speaks of the huge popularity won by the thick black composition, which the Egyptians from the beginning of the III millennium BC embalmed the bodies of the deceased. The demand for it was very large, and the solidified mass started being cleaned from skulls and bone residues, scraped from body cavities and processed. Entrepreneurial merchants hired peasants to excavate necropoles and set up exports. As a result the "amber at from the tombs" in the XIV – XV centuries became a common medium sold in pharmacies and shops.

And that's where the most interesting thing starts! Raw materials began to be missed. And instead of ancient mummies, "fresh" went into the case. The torturers made a lot from selling corpses right from the scaffold. The washers of Egyptian scumbags were stolen from the graves of the bodies just buried, and, according to I. P. Neumyvakin, "dismembered them and digested them in boilers until the muscles separated from the bones; The oily liquid dripped from the boiler and, spilled into the flakes, was sold for furious money to the franc merchants." The Navarra physician Guy de la Fontaine testified in 1564 that piles of slave bodies intended for processing into an "improved" mummy had been found in the warehouse of one of the mumie traders in Alexandria.

This madness had been going on for centuries! And not in gray antiquity, but in quite enlightened times. In 1694, Pierre Pome, a Parisian merchant and merchant of apothecary goods, in his work

"The Universal History of Apothecary Affairs", attempted to discourage people from using mummies, painting on engravings a disgusting way of processing corpses. However, this did not have the necessary impact on the public.

Corpses were actively used for medical purposes. The above mentioned Crollius recommended human flesh as a drug, primarily an antidote. It had to be held for a few days in wine alcohol, and then dried. Further, the author explained, the pharmacist will once again need wine alcohol to restore the flesh to a natural red hue. Since the appearance of the corpse is unappetized, it should have been soaked in olive oil for a month. The oil contains useful substances from the mummy, and it could be used for medicinal purposes as well. *(cannibalism?)*

A famous French chemist and pharmacist of the 17th century Nicolas Lefevre somewhat modernized the formulation. To begin with, he wrote, it is necessary to cut off muscles from the corpse of a healthy and young man, to let them wash in wine alcohol, then to hang in a dry cool place. If the air is wet or it rains, these muscles need to be dried on a weak fire from juniper to the state of corned beef which was eaten by sailors.

However, we should not be surprised by the tolerance of European peers to such recipes. Mores during the Middle Ages, Renaissance, Enlightenment were in many of their manifestations so ludicrous that we can only astonish when looking back.

Here is one of the episodes, so to speak, of the city chronicle of Paris. This is going to be an "incident" involving the corpse of Marshal d 'Ancra, the Italian-hard-line adventurist Conchino Conchini, the favorite of Queen Maria Medici, the wife of Henry IV and the mother of Louis XIII (on the orders of the latter the marshal-favorite was killed). On the morning of April 25, 1617, the poorest Parisian stormed the doors of the church of Saint-Germain-l' Oxerroix, where this never fought and extremely unsolicited marshal was wounded.

Having pulled the body from under the grave plate, the crowd tied the corpse of the leg with a rope detached from the tongue of the bell, dragged it through the streets and the embankment and hung its head down, either on one of the gallows (which were an important part of the urban landscape) or on the support of the New Bridge. But it was also not enough for the infuriated Parisians. Someone cut off the ears, nose and penis of the corpse with an acutely filled knife. Soon the remains were dragged around Paris again. And finally, having returned to the New Bridge, threw in the divorced immediately fire. Some citizen opened the chest and, having ripped out the heart, slightly eased on fire, swallowed. Curtain...

By the way, by this time Europe was already well acquainted with the phenomenon of cannibalism. It became an inevitable companion to the famine that periodically engulfed the continent. The worst was the great famine of 1314-1315. The summer of 1314 was rainy, and a year later a real flood broke out. The result was a catastrophic crop failure and... High demand for human flesh.

The chronicle monk Raul Glaber gives emotional evidence of European cannibalism in 1032-1034: "...having quickly destroyed animals and birds, people began to eat the dead and all kinds of things that are scary to mention... A real hunt began: travellers who fled hunger were stopped on the roads, killed, cut apart and fried. Others were killed and eaten at night by those who provided them with overnight accommodation. The children, having seen from afar a bait in the form of an egg or apple, ran in hopes of receiving food, and became food themselves. The worst part was that people began to like the taste of human flesh. They even dug up recently buried corpses... Someone thought it possible to reach the end in this terrible logic: this man began to sell boiled human meat on the market. However, this turned out to be too much: he was grabbed and burned alive. The terrible goods were buried in the ground; Some hungry one excavated it and ate it, however, discovered at the crime scene, was also captured and burned. The same punishment was imposed on the "wild man" something like an ogre, who was rampant in the forest of Shatne in Makon Province. He arranged for himself a dwelling near the secluded, but apparently often visited my church. Those who asked for him for a night out or just walked past

his house were doomed. He had already eaten 48 victims whose severed heads rot in his hut when one of the passers-by, who was stronger than him, managed to escape. The Earl of Otton, having learned of what happened from this saved man, gathered all the people he could have. The cannibal was captured, brought to Macon, tied to a bone in a barn. Monks from nearby Cranie saw him roasting on a bonfire with their own eyes..."

Maniac experimenters

The search for prototypes of Grenouille will lead us in much later times, namely the 1950s. Galicia, an autonomous province in Spain, was agitated by the trial of Manuel Blanco Romasanta. He was exposed as a serial killer of women and children. In addition, there are reasons to believe that Romasanta refreshed his victims, pumped out fat from corpses, and he was already sold to pharmacies, who produced high-quality soap from this raw material. Curiously, the defendant, without denying committing the murders, nevertheless refused to admit guilt. He said at the trial that he had been taken possession of the amazing disease "licantropia" which turned a person into a wolf.

Following the trial, the psychopath maniac was sentenced to death by strangulation. The case was then transferred to the court of the highest instance, which noticed the execution with life imprisonment. A retributed prosecutor, certainly supported by the public, appealed the decision. And as a result of the new hearings, the original sentence was restored: strangle the bastard.

But ... The mighty of this world interfered. Queen Isabella II of Spain was approached by a French doctor who wanted to explore a wolf man. So Romasanta was saved from the gallows - the monastic actually cancelled the execution. Further events beyond years are not possible to restore. Romasanta either died in prison or escaped it and disappeared... And in the 20th and 21st centuries he became a hero of books and films.

It is known that some scientists from the German Nazis experimented with human fat to produce perfumery and hygiene products. There is an indication of this in the materials of the Nuremberg Trial, where the leaders of the Third Reich were tried. Here is the record of the witness's interrogation.

"On May 28, 1945, Danzburg, Military Prosecutor of the Rear of the 2nd Belarusian Front, Lieutenant Colonel of Justice Geitman and Military Investigator of the Military Prosecutor's Office of the 2nd Belarusian Front, Major of Justice Kadensky questioned the below listed witness, who provided testimony of the following:

Mazur Sigmund Yuzefovich,

Born in 1920, a native of Danzburg, he took German nationality in January 1944. Graduated from 6 grades of Polish gymnasium in Danzburg in 1939, served voluntarily in 1939 in the Polish army, former official, single, no prior convictions, lived in Danzburg, Bechergasse, No. 2, position until April 1945 - anatomist of the anatomical institute of Danzburg, Has a mother in Danzburg, Neishotland Street, No. 10, speaks Polish and German. The witness made this statement knowing that he might be prosecuted for perjury if the statement were known by him to be false and was intended by him to mislead.

The translator is aware that it is an offence to refuse to translate and for giving false translation under articles 92, 95 of the Criminal Code of the RSFSR.

In October 1940, while in Danzburg, I was looking for a job. The German official Gustav Lange of the working bureau of Danzburg, to whom I gave one room from my apartment, promised me to find a better, more suitable job in some educational institution of Danzburg, after which I was sent to the anatomical institute of

Danzburg, where I began working in January 1941. I first worked as a courier for three months. Working as a courier, I became interested in medicine and with the help of Lange and Professor Spanner I was appointed to the position of the anatomist of the anatomical institute since January 1941. My duties as an anatomist included drawing tables and helping to autopsy corpses.

The director of the anatomical institute was a German from Kiel, Professor Spanner Rudolf, who left for a neighborhood of the city of Halle in January 1945.

Spanner's deputy professor was Dr. Associate Professor Woolman - an SS officer, but he used to wear civilian clothes and sometimes a black SS uniform. Volman is from Czechoslovakia, his Czechoslovak surname is Kozlik. he voluntarily joined the SS troops in January 1945. The assistant since October 1944 had been a woman, Fosbeck from Tsoppot, who left for Halle with Professor Spanner. She assisted Professor Spanner. The senior producer was von Bargen, who came to Danzburg from Kiel with Professor Spanner. The attendant who carried the bodies was a German named Reichert from Danzburg, who left in November 1944 for the German army. There was one more attendant, a German named Borkman from Danzburg, but I have no idea where he is now.

Question: Tell us how soap was made from human fat at the anatomical institute of Danzburg.

Answer: A stone one-story building of three rooms was built near the anatomical institute deep in the yard in the summer of 1943. The mentioned building was erected for the treatment of corpses, the digestion of bones. This was announced by Professor Spanner. This laboratory was called a laboratory for making skeletons of human and burning meat and unnecessary bones. But already in the winter of 1943-1944 Professor Spanner ordered to collect human fat and not to throw it away. This order was given to Reichert and Borkman.

In February 1944, Professor Spanner gave me a recipe for making soap from human fat. In this recipe it was prescribed to take 5 kilos of human fat with 10 litres of water and 500 or 1000 g of caustic soda, after that cook all these for 2-3 hours, then let cool. The soap floats up and residues and water remains at the bottom in buckets. A handful of table salt and soda was added to the mixture. Fresh water was then added and the mixture was again cooked for 2-3 hours. After cooling, the ready soap was poured into molds.

The soap turned out to be of unpleasant smell. Benzaldehyde was added to destroy this unpleasant smell.

The operation of making soap from human fat began in January 1944. The direct chief of the soap factory was the senior anatomist von Bargen. All the equipment was taken from the anatomical institute.

The first batch of corpses was delivered from Conradstein from a psychiatric hospital, the exact number I do not remember. In addition, there was a large supply of corpses at the anatomical institute in the amount of about 400 corpses. Most of the corpses were decapitated. The decapitated bodies were delivered after being guillotined in Kenigsberg prison, and in 1944 the guillotine was installed in Danzburg prison. I saw this guillotine in one of the prison rooms, and I saw it when I went to Danzburg prison for corpses. I attach the scheme of the guillotine.

When I came to prison for corpses, the corpses were fresh, just after the execution, and we took them in the room next to the one where the guillotine was coming. The bodies were still warm. For each corpse there was a card with the name and year of birth, and these names in the anatomical institute fit into the axial book. Where this book is now, I don't know. I went to prison for corpses in Danzburg about 4 or 5 times.

Struthof Borkman brought 4 Russian people, males, from the concentration camp. Fat was collected by Borkman and Reichert. The soap was cooked by me from the corpses of men and women. One production cook took several days - from 3 to 7 days. Of the two processes of cooking known to me, in which I was directly involved, we got more than 25 kilograms of soap product, and 70-80 kilograms of human fat. About 40 bodies, were collected for these processes. The ready soap came to Professor Spanner, who kept it by himself in person.

The production of soap from human bodies, as I know, was of interest for Hitler's government. The Minister of Education Rust, Minister of Health Conti, gauleiter of Danzburg Albert Forster, as well as many other professors from other medical institutes came to the anatomical institute.

Personally, I used this soap for my needs, for toilet and laundry. Personally, I took four kilos for this soap. Since this soap production rout was made at the behest of Professor Spanner, I found it normal. Reichert, Borkman, von Bargen and our chief professor Spanner, as well as all other employees also took the soap for themselves. Some students who assisted in the work were also given this soap. Professor Spanner said that the production of soap from human fat should be kept secret.

We have an experimental soap preparation at the institute, but when it was supposed to use corpses for the making of soap on a large scale, I don 't know. Professor Spanner tried to get as many corpses as possible and engaged in correspondence with prisons and concentration camps with which he agreed that the corpses in these places were booked by the Danzig Anatomical Institute. The incoming corpses were shrouded in the lab, and the hair was burned, in any case the facts of hair use are not known to me. Just like human fat, Professor Spanner ordered the collection of human skin, which, after degreasing, was treated with certain chemicals. The production of human skin was carried out by the senior anatomist von Bargen and Professor Spanner himself. The worked out skin was folded into boxes and was used for special purposes, but which ones, I don't know.

At the anatomical institute there were conferences of scientific composition, and I know there were three conferences of this kind, but what was discussed at them, I cannot say, as I did not attend them.

Written in my words, translated for me into Polish and verified by me.

Signature: Masur Siegmund."

Finally, it should be added that Professor of Medicine Rudolf Maria Spanner was never brought to trial for what he did and died in his bed in 1960 at the age of 65. During the Nuremberg trial, the Soviet prosecuting attorney tried to use the activities of the Anatomical Institute in Danzburg as one of the evidences of the crimes of Nazism against humanity, but did not receive support. Moreover, three years before his death Rudolf Spanner headed the Cologne Anatomical Institute and created an anatomical atlas there, which is well known to specialists and still used. Did the professor regret making soap from people? Was his remorse tormented? We don't know anything about that.

CHAPTER II.

Did They Really Stink So Badly?

People stank of sweat and unwashed clothes; from their mouths came the stench of rotting teeth, from their bellies that of onions, and from their bodies, if they were no longer very young, came the stench of rancid cheese and sour milk and tumorous disease. The rivers stank, the marketplaces stank, the churches stank, it stank beneath the bridges and in the palaces. The peasant stank as did the priest, the apprentice as did his master's wife, the whole of the aristocracy stank, even the king himself stank, stank like a rank lion, and the queen like an old goat, summer and winter.

Patrick Süskind.

"Perfume: The story of a murderer"

Do you remember the shock you experienced when you first read "Perfume"? It is not the escapades of the glamorous killer Jean-Baptiste Grenouille that I am talking about; the residents of modern megacities have got quite used to such things. Any investigator on particularly important cases can tell stories of far more terrifying nature.

The most shocking were most unpleasant smells and unsanitary which accompanied the life of the ancestors of modern Europeans. Not such remote ancestors, by the way: from the times described in Patrick Süskind's book ten generations had not yet replaced each other. What is true in this description, and what is artistic fiction? There are exactly the opposite opinions on this. And supporters of each version refer to their sources.

Let's start with the one that is quite consistent with Süskind 's text.

Kings and bast wisp

If you introduce me to a man who associates historical periods with the names of great artists, musicians or scientists, I will long and sincerely shake his hand, melting compliments to a unique worldview. For most people any historical era is first of all the history of leadership: kings, emperors, sultans, shahs, presidents and SG's. It is easier to perceive and remember historical epochs this way. Let us not forget about the upsetting toadyism accompanying humanity for many centuries: the habits of the monarch immediately became common in his surroundings to begin with and then in the wider circles of the managerial elite. The decisive parting with beards under Peter I and the endemic fascination with tennis of Yeltsin officials are phenomena of the same order.

Therefore, speaking of hygiene, sanitary conditions of our Western neighbors usually begin with crowned persons.

Some European rulers smelled nausea. You would not stand next to them for a couple of minutes. Many homeless people would spot the smell of such a ruler of a European country.

The royal personalities smelled at all with the recommendations of the croakers of those times. Known to us, as an "augur" Michel Nostradamus (1503-1566) deserves much more respect as a smart lecturer who effectively fought the plague, as well as a propagandist of basic hygienic procedures. The title of one of his books (copies are preserved in Paris libraries) sounds as follows: "An excellent and very useful brochure about many excellent recipes, divided into two parts. The first part of it teaches how to prepare different pomades and perfumes for face decoration. The second part of us teaches how to cook jam of various varieties from honey, sugar and wine. Compiled by Master Michel Nostradamus - Doctor of Medicine from Salon in Provence. Lyon 1572."

Nostradamus writes about such things as: how to cook tooth powder, how to make your breath smell in a pleasant way, how to clean one's teeth, even badly spoiled rot, how to make soap making hands white and soft, how to destroy. However, this book never became a best-seller. Completely different medical advice were in fashion.

For example, the personal doctor of English King Edward II John Gatisden at the end of the 13th century recommended as a procedure for preserving the integrity of teeth to breathe their own excreta (and this is many centuries after the ancient Romans, who prepared powder from thick pearls or coral for cleaning teeth!).

The author of the XV century popular medical tract of deep thought - but claimed that water weakens the body and expands pores on the skin, and there can penetrate the air infected with maladies. Therefore, the washed person can get sick or even die.

Another leading light in medicine, already in the XVI century, especially warned against washing the face: even more - it causes catarrh and impairs vision! Ridiculously? No! The reason for all these misconceptions was the Great Epidemic of the Plague of 1348. It set the stage for quite logical ideas in general that all diseases, each of which at that time could become deadly, live in sinister air and water, and at any moment are able to break into the body.

Should we be surprised that monarchs that were well aware of the achievements of modern medicine treated water procedures with shame?

From a French historian Philip Erlanger's book "The Age of Yards and Kings. Etiquette and customs. 1558-1715" we learn that King Jacob I of England and Scotland (1566-1625) never washed his hands, only wetting his fingertips with a wet napkin. Queen Isabella of Castile (1451-1504), under whose reign Christopher Columbus discovered America and the "holy" Inquisition appeared, remained a woman of outstanding beauty and virtue in the memories of contemporaries. Another fact is of particular interest to us is that Isabella of Castile gave a vow not to wash herself or change her undergarment until Spain wins over Granada.

Month after month, the snow-white royal color was gradually dilapidated, becoming greyish-yellow. The Spanish have since referred to this "exquisite" shade as "color Isabel". Legend says that obtaining permission and money for the Columbus's expedition was easier because he approached Queen Isabella at a distance of 5 meters and valiantly sustained a 20-minute audience, without giving away his disgust.

What thoughts about the vow did the royal spouse Ferdinand of Aragon have? History is silent. Note that the exemplary Catholic queen spent a lot of time hiking, sitting on a horse, which most likely added new smelling notes to the royal stench.

Speaking of the famous King Henry IV (he was Henry of Navarro, 1553-1610), the very thing that, saying "Paris stands Mass" broke with Protestants and became Catholic, thus opening the way to the French throne, it is said that he washed himself only three times in his life. By the way, Henry who despised hygiene had a reputation of a true Lothario, which characterizes not only him, but also the unpretentious court ladies.

In the diary of Jean Erouard, the personal physician of Henry 's son, the future Louis XIII, who had followed him since his birth in September 1601, there are many details about the hygiene standards kept for the small dauphin. "On 11 November 1601, his head was first rubbed. On 17 November 1601, his forehead and face were rubbed with fresh butter and almond milk as dirt appeared there. On July 4, 1602, he had his hair combed, he liked it, and he turned his head where he was scratching. On 3 October 1606, he had his feet washed with warm water for the first time. On August 2, 1608, he took his first bath."

By the way, it is necessary to pay tribute to Louis XIII (1601-1643), whose role in the TV film about musketeers was performed by Oleg Tabakov. He was just, despite unsanitary infancy and malevolent surroundings, a man of pure density, and by the standards of his times a real neatnik. Every morning he took baths, washed his feet. As a three-year-old prince, Louis, passing from Saint-Germain Castle to Paris through the suburbs of Saint-Honoré - a new and far better ventilated quarter than the inner-city ancient quarters - immediately felt the veil shake from the waters of the brook along which the carriage was moving, and flung his nose.

"Mamanga!" He said, addressing her governess, Madame de Mongla. "How bad it smells!"

The baby was immediately given a handkerchief soaked in vinegar. Later, having already become an adult, Louis was tormented by the smell coming to his windows from the ditches surrounding the Louvre, and constantly tried to escape from the city towards the open nature.

Sometimes doctors, despite their generally unsanitary activity, still benefit the decaying monarchs in the mud. They insisted several times on the washing of another French king, Louis XIV (1638-1715). However, the glorified King-Sun, who reigned for more than 70 years and condemned the legendary "State is me!" did not appreciate the efforts of doctors. Apparently, due to the devilish craze of water, bringing objective pleasure, but at the same time ominously expanding pores and deteriorating vision, he hardly ever visited the bathroom.

Many ladies and gentlemen, counts, dukes, marquises and barons fully matched their stinky lords. They washed themselves infrequently and smelled, apparently, pretty much the same as their king.

There is a historical anecdote about a certain Duke of Norfolk who refused to wash himself out of religious beliefs (we will talk about the impact of Christianity on medieval hygiene later). The man was voluntarily rotting alive. His body was almost completely covered with purulent, and his servants could not stand it. They waited for the Duke to drink himself unconscious and, without asking permission, washed his lordship's body. Of course, it is nothing more than a curious incident. Most aristocrats sought to rid themselves and others of the smell of an unwashed body. They used over-dried rags, special powder, bags with smelling herbs worn in folds of clothes (they are extant and known as sachets).

Handkerchiefs (Italian fazzoletto) went in fashion, seemingly decorative, but with them ladies and gentlemen could drive away the flies who sat down on their dirty bodies.

And what happened to the hair! Those who were more victorious and could not afford powder to achieve fashion blond sprinkled unwashed hair with chalk and flour (the latter gave the necessary lush). Lard was used everywhere to create volume to the hair. All this was a paradise for parasites, whom beautiful women with different success tried to expel with the help of a special long stick. Fleas and microbes could reproduce kind in the folds of clothing: expensive garments made of velvet and brocade were hardly ever cleaned except by gentle beating. It is not by chance that the noble lady of the XVI-XVIII centuries did not break up with the "fleabag". Its functions at different times and in different countries were performed by precious brooches, inside which there was a mixture of blood and honey, a miniature fork with movable tine, pieces of fur or fur handbags. The living fleabags were small dogs, as well as weasels, ferrets and martens.

The hygienic nightmare in which the kings and their retinue were living was exacerbated by the unsanitary state that prevailed in the palaces. Such a concept as "toilet" in the modern sense of the word did not exist even in the celebrated residences of French kings. Not only servants, but also highborn inhabitants of the Louvre did number two in yards, on the stairs, on the balconies. Apparently, the concepts of what is embarrassing were very different from the current ones. The court and sovereigns did the deed on the sills by the open windows. And only some neatniks preferred night vases, the contents of which was poured outside the gate of the palace. For the same purposes, the walls were covered with drapes and alcoves were made in the corridors. The rough, unclean food that even aristocrats fed on made diarrhea something not off-the-wall, not an emerging event, but a common, everyday phenomenon. So drapes and alcoves were never empty.

Given by Charles V (1338-1380) in 1364, the instruction to paint the garden and corridors of the Louvre with red crosses to stop those wishing to use the palace premises as a toilet remained a fine and naive attempt to avoid the inevitable.

The famous memoirist Duke de Saint-Simon (1675-1755) left to his descendants a detailed description of mores and life at the court of Louis XIV. In particular, the memoirs of the Duke describe the court ladies of Versailles who did the deed pretty much in the middle of a small talk.

Years passed, fashion trends, architectural styles, technologies of production of goods changed. But something remained unchanged. In the mid-18th century, a memoirist described the flavors of the Palace of Versailles: "Parks, gardens and the castle itself are disgusting due to their scorn stink. The aisles, yards, buildings and corridors are filled with urine and feces; near the phase where the ministers live the butcher kills and roasts the pigs every morning; and the whole street of Saint-Clou is filled with rotten water and covered with dead cats."

Having made a mess out of one palace, kings and their retinue moved to the next castle, giving servants the opportunity to ventilate the premises and remove the waste.

It would seem clear. But there is also an alternative view on the sanitary and hygienic state of old Europe.

And yet they did wash themselves!

Starting from the 15th century, solid soap was produced en masse in Europe. At the same time animal fats were connected not with wood ash of the fire, as before, but with natural calcined soda. This significantly reduced the cost of soap, transferred soap from artisanal production to manufacturing production. Soap became available to any person of middle wealth and, especially, to any representative of a rich nobility. You would agree that it would be strange to increase the output of products for which there were no demand. So, consumers bought and used the goods: washed their clothes and washed themselves. Probably less often than now, but the citizens of the 18th and earlier centuries simply did not need to wash as often as our contemporaries do. After all, the ecological state of cities, not damaged by smoke pipes of factories and plants, was much more favorable for the human organism. In addition, synthetic food supplements have not yet been invented...

The above-mentioned Louis XIII was not the only neatnik-monarch. As the eldest daughter of the Prussian king Friedrich Wilhelm I (1688-1740) Wilhelmine said, her dad washed himself "almost twenty times a day", rubbed his hands constantly, "and his rooms had to be so clean and tidy that there was no dust anywhere left." Friedrich Wilhelm I found a radical solution to the lice problem, forcing his entourage (and these were in the basic military) to shave bald and wear wigs... In the memories of Wilhelmine, who took a special attitude from her father to purity, an assessment of the hygienicity of certain historic figures is often given. For example, she writes that when her brother's bride was brought to the palace, Prussian princesses were unhappily surprised at how bad she smelled...

In various sources it is possible to find information that calls into question the notion of court ladies of the Middle Ages and the "Galant Age" as "dirty creatures". For example, the uncorroborated Queen of France, Louis XV 's favourite and mistress Marquis de Pompadour had a bidet made of fine wood, with inlays and gilded bronze linings. It should be mentioned that this is the same Louis XV who (as Süskind puts it) "stunk like a wild beast."

Moreover,in the case of Louis XIV not every fact is so obvious. Yeah, he didn't like washing himself. However, there is evidence that the king changed his undergarments several times a day and that he was regularly rubbed from head to toe with perfumed lotion (this procedure was traditional for nobles).

Ladies taking baths was one of the common fine arts plots. In the mid-16th century, another uncorroborated queen of France - Henry II's mistress Diana de Poitiers – sat for the painter and graphic of François Clue right during the saponification. The result was the painting "Lady in the Bathroom" which is now stored in the Washington National Gallery. A little later, in the late 16th century, an unknown artist captured in the bathroom the favorite of French King Henry IV Gabriel d 'Estre with her sister. Keep in mind that this is the same Henry IV who kind of washed himself only three times in his life... Something doesn't quite add up here, am I right? Could the famous monarch have been maligned? The rich citizens in the bathrooms were portrayed by the famous French painter, Grenouille's "peer" Jean Michel Moro Jr., as well as the artist Jean-Baptiste Pater, who lived half a century earlier.

The baths themselves began to be produced in Europe for personal use, replacing basins and pitchers in houses, around the 17th century. In history remained the entrepreneurial French Level, the manufacturer of metal containers for washing, as well as columns for heating water. Later, sedentary baths – "boots" in which hot water remained for quite a long time, became common. It was in such a boot that the ideologist of the French Revolution Marat was killed, and this happened a few decades after Süskind described bloody expositions of Jean-Baptiste Grenouille.

The truth is in the middle

So did the kings and others stink or didn't they? What version is truthful? To answer these questions you should understand that, speaking of hygiene in Europe, completely different periods are often mixed up.

The collapse of the Roman Empire with its bath tracts did not completely destroy the European's washing habits and hygiene procedures. Many terms built by the Romans in different parts of Europe continued to work, somewhere they built new ones - in their image and likeness. In the 13th-16th centuries, public baths could be found in every more or less large city.

They didn't go to the bath just to wash themselves. Immediately the clients had their hair cut and shaved, and had their bodies massaged. The level of bath establishments was not the same, prices per visit also varied. Therefore, water procedures were available to both the poor and the rich. Even in roadside hotels, the guest could find a soap and clean himself up. The rich and aristocrats, of course, preferred to wash themselves without leaving the house. They were supplied with water for a fee by street aquifers.

Therefore, the Middle Ages was not a period of comprehensive mud. By no means. The only problems were with oral hygiene. Toothpastes and powders came to Europe much later. Special rinsing solutions were not widely available. Thus, the tooth-drawers had no shortage of clientele.

But already at the end of the 16th century the sanitary situation of Europe deteriorated. By the time Louis XIV reigned, there were virtually no public baths left in the capital of France.

One reason for this is the gradual reduction of the average annual temperature. Harsh and prolonged winters have become usual for Europe. The "Small Ice Age" lasted for several centuries and led to massive deforestation. Prices for firewood, and therefore the cost of visiting the baths increased. Nevertheless, it was not the wood and its prices that was the reason. It appears that many public baths also functioned as informal brothels, and saponification was only an addition to adult services. It was officially frowned upon. For example, the regulations for Paris bankers dating from the 13th century explicitly state that they should not turn their establishments into brothels. However, as the German mores researcher Edward Fuchs wrote in the early 20th century, "the role of bath-house attendants was usually performed by prostitutes. The names "banter" and "prostitute" were synonymous. To call a woman a "banter" was considered a terrible insult."

The perception of baths, as places of immoral nature, has partly shifted to the attitude towards hygiene as such. But this, like the rise in wood prices, was not the main reason for the death of bath culture.

Rampant bath life was an inexhaustible occasion for jokes, wit and satirical drawings.

The fear of infecting with an incurable disease was crucial. We've already mentioned the plague. In addition to it in Europe syphilis was rioting. It spread across the continent after the return of Columbus's ships from America. Syphilis killed many millions of people in a matter of decades. No one even thought of going to public baths that had a reputation of brothels and, besides, were getting more expensive each year. People thought it was better to be not too clean but at least alive.

As a result, it can be assumed that in the Middle Ages, Renaissance and Enlightenment, different patterns of attitudes towards hygiene and sanitation actually coexisted on an equal footing among privileged classes. There was no generally accepted norm per se. That is why proponents of contradictory versions find arguments so easily.

It is unlikely that rich and noble people were stinky slovens. But the same bath was seen by many as a luxury item and a place of relaxation rather than an acute hygienic necessity. Besides, the object is not quite safe and not too decent. And this is certainly true when it comes to common people.

A lot depended, obviously, on the human factor, including the factor of the king, who defined the mores in his court. Let us revisit the memories of Wilhelmine of Prussia, struck by the unpleasant smell of her brother 's bride. The hygiene at the Prussian court was at an unaffordable height for the rest of Europe, so the "provincial girl" (Elizabeth Christina, daughter of the Duke of Brunswick-Lüneburg-Wolfenbüttel) did seem very untidy.

The poor were much less concerned with these hygienic passions. They had no money for soap, baths or changes of underwear. Lived as always, smelled as always... Washed themselves infrequently, probably in rivers. And hardly thought it to be a big deal.

Lice-ridden religious teachers

The role of dominant Western European Catholicism in sanitation and hygiene is considered almost decisive. Is it really so? It is unlikely. It is hard to imagine that for an average European, holy fathers' prescriptions were more important than the above mentioned syphilis or plague. So the role of Christian pastors was, probably, minor. However, it would be wrong to deny that they did play some part in people's lives.

The word and the deed in the church, as is often the case in influential organizations claiming ideological leadership, did not fully match each other.

At first about words. In the church, there has long been a concept of the killing of tiny flesh as opposed to the care of the soul. As Pope Gregory the Great used to say (540-604), the body is a nasty dress of the soul. And if so - to improve it (the body) via cleaning procedures is truly stupid. Of course, it was, among other things, a polemic attack against the "immoral pagans" from ancient Rome, who loved to spend time in terms.

Christians were strictly forbidden to wash in a bath with the Jews. Rule No. 11 of the Quinisext Council (691-692) stated that "none of those belonging to the Holy Rank or of the laity shall by any means yell desalination, given by the Jews, or join in communion with them, neither in diseases to call upon them, nor doctors to accept from them, nor in baths bathed with them. If whoever dares to do this: then the cleric will be erupted, and the layman will be excommunicated." But how to protect yourself from such "sedition"? In the bath-house there is truly no rich, poor, Greel, or Jewish - just naked people. So it's better to avoid visiting these baths at all, to get out of harm's way.

Particular irritation among church figures was caused by the tradition of men and women attending public baths together in some parts of Europe.

Washing was also dangerous because it was possible to wash off the holy water to which it touched at baptism. This was written by the creator of the canonical Latin text of the Bible, St. Jerome (IV- V centuries). With his inherent fiery temperament and radicalism, he rejected hygiene in principle, because the rite of baptism laundered a Christian once and for all.

"Purity was viewed with disgust. Lice were called "God 's pearls" and were considered a sign of holiness. Saints, both male and female, usually quipped that the water never touched their feet, except when they had to cross a river," writes an English philosopher Bertrand Russell.

Of course, words alone were not enough. They needed to be confirmed by practical examples. And the Church generated the corresponding examples. It also had its own "dukes of Norfolk." These are shutters such as St. Simeon of Syracuse (died 1035). The life of this amazing person age is worthy of at least a brief description. Simeon 's father, a Greek from Sicily, moved to Constantinople when the boy was seven years old. After reaching adulthood, Simeon went to Palestine. He first lived as a hermit in the Jordan Valley, then took a monastic at a monastery in Bethlehem and finally moved into an abode at the foot of Sinai. With the permission of the rector, he lived for two years as a hermit in a cave near the Red Sea, and then moved to the top of Mount Sinai itself. The rector soon sent him to Normandy, to Duke Richard II, who promised the monastery a major donation. Pirates captured the ship, but Simeon managed to jump into the sea and swam to the shore. With incredible difficulties, Simeon reached Rouen, however by that time the duke had died, and his successor said he did not wish to sacrifice anything.

Simeon did not want to return to the monastery empty-handed and, with the permission of the bishop that he had met during his journey, settled as a gate in Trier (the homeland of Karl Marx). The Bishop gave him a tower near the gate, since called Simeon's Gate. The locals, because of his unusual appearance and speech, felt that the alien was a sorcerer; Simeon's keel was attacked in an attempt to kill him; luckily, the doors were firmly locked for both him and the attackers. Over time, however, the locals began to honor him as a saint and a miracle worker, and seven years after his death he was solemnly recognized as a saint.

There is one wonderful place in his life that cannot be bypassed in the context of our subject. The man clogged himself alive in the tower. Something was to eat, modest, but still... His food was sifted into the window. Sat in his turret for a few years idly... You can imagine what was going on in this crypt. The main part of the body, sacrificed by St. Simeon, was to be his own nose.

The founder of the Order of Friars Minor Francis of Assise appeared before the Pope in such a pathetic form that he failed: "Go, my son, to the pigs; you seem to have more in common with them than with people; knock in the mud and exercise them in your sermons." Francis immediately went to the pigs and then reappeared to the pope. Affected by his humility, the head of the church gave him the right to preach in temples.

The history of Catholicism knows other persons who claimed to be moral authorities, who permanently humbled their flesh, who cultivated strict asceticism. Some of them stuffed themselves in tombs, repeating and even surpassing the "feat" of St. Simeon.

People talked of the likes of Saint Benedict of Anyan, the reformer of the Benedictine Order (c. 745/750-821) with prevailing respect: "A lot of lice were crawling about his rough skin, devouring his body exhausted by fasts."

Apparently, the literal perception of lice as "God's pearls" predetermined the exotic procedure of electing the mayor in the medieval town of Gurdenburg, Sweden. If there were several honourable citizens applying for high office, candidates would sit around the table and lay their beards on it. Then the "referee" threw a louse in the middle of the table. The winner was the applicant whose beard was chosen by the insect.

A French Catholic historian of the early 18th century, Antoine Calme, lists with approval the evidence of mistrust of the monastic orders in hygiene. The Cistercians excommunicated someone who washed without permission. Cartesian people were forbidden to swim in rivers and ponds. The monks of Monte Cassino, the oldest abbey of the Benedictine order, founded in 529 by St. Benedict himself, were allowed to wash themselves only in extreme cases, for which the permission of the general surrender - the supreme council - was required! The elderly monks of Bursfeld 's congregation (religious association) took a bath four times a year and the young ones twice a year. The monks of the Benedictine monastery of Girsau washed themselves twice a year. Elsewhere they washed for Christmas, Easter and Pentecost. Only the sick had the right to wash their bodies when necessary.

Some sources indicate that the charter of St. Clarisse's Catholic nunnery in Munich strictly prohibited the nuns from using paper after visiting the latrine. Perhaps this is an anti-Catholic provocation and such a ban did not exist in nature. Perhaps. But if it was so, this ban had substance.

The body of St. Thomas Beckett, Archbishop of Canterbury, who was killed in 1170, I was remembered by the contemporary as a habitation of parasites. A large brown mantle was on the corpse; under it was a white stun; then three wool coats, then the black rob of the Benedictines, a usual shirt. Since the body was already cold, the parasites that lived in this multi-layered clothing began to crawl out in the hundreds in front of the silent observers.

However, it would be unfair to refer to the Catholic cleric as a commonwealth of cherished nations. The faith teachers who died their flesh were inferior in number to persons of a completely different nature.

Let us recall the brilliant political leader Cardinal de Richelieu, who, despite the priestly garb and celibacy, had many love affairs with the noble ladies of France. Or let's look at another great cardinal politician - Jules Mazarin- who managed to conquer the heart of the widow of King Louis III of Austria. Or the evil Roman Pope Alexander VI (Borgia) - legendary poisoner, bribetaker and debauchee of the 15th century. Or many other high priests of the Middle Ages and later epochs, distinguished from Signor Borgia only by the number of mistresses, illegitimate children and the level of cynicism. Or hundreds of holy fathers who received church office and priorate for money (even a special term was coined for this phenomenon – "simony").

Will someone seriously assure that these famous and little-known people in priestly garbs have not washed themselves for years and rejoiced insects in their clothes? Of course, no.

The following conclusion can be drawn from the above. Certain religious fanatics, heirs of St. Jerome, rejecting hygienic procedures, could influence their inner circle and part of the flock. But it would be wrong to blame Catholicism for requiring Europeans to walk around dirty, stinky and lice-driven.

However, the fight against cats declared by the church to be the devil incarnate got medieval Europe in lots of troubles. These animals were considered the first assistants of witches, who themselves, as believed, could turn into a black cat. Cats were tanked, dropped from towers, burned on the bonfires of the Inquisition in hundreds. In Holland, a special "Cat Wednesday", the day of mass extermination of cats was established. The result of the mouse-catcher's persecution was that rats spread with astonishing speed throughout the continent, which in turn provoked horrible plague epidemics.

CHAPTER III.

Is It True That Cities Were Drowning In Mud?

In the period of which we speak, there reigned in the cities a stench barely conceivable to us modern men and women. The streets stank of manure, the courtyards of urine, the stairwells stank of moldering wood and rat droppings, the kitchens of spoiled cabbage and mutton fat; the unaired parlors stank of stale dust, the bedrooms of greasy sheets, damp featherbeds, and the pungently sweet aroma of chamber pots. The stench of sulfur rose from the chimneys, the stench of caustic lyes from the tanneries, and from the slaughterhouses came the stench of congealed blood.

Patrick Süskind.

"Perfume: The story of a murderer"

While the courtiers were entertaining themselves in the gated castles, and the furious monks were tormenting their own rotting flesh, European cities were drowning in mud together with residents of all classes, sexes and ages. There can be no two opinions here anymore.

Residents of medieval cities held small cattle - goats, sheep, and pigs were not kicked out of the city; they found abundant food - organic garbage. During the rains, the streets turned into swamps in which the cart and equestrians were stuck. When there were no rains, was impossible to breathe because of caustic and evil dust.

Are you longing to go to Paris?

Süskind described the Paris entourage quite alive and truthfully. By the way, it was stinky Paris, that became one of the main heroes of "Perfume", that could rightly be considered the capital of European sewage.

Venomous drain ditches emitted "at the same time a cadaverous and hell-giving sulphur smell, which, as the contemporaries said, "was more aggressive than mustard." This way the French historian Emile Mans describes them, talking about Paris of the early 17th century. If the street was wide enough, there were two parallel stink rolls flowing through it in special troughs, on the narrow street the rugs were alone. The central Paris streets, all of these St Antoine, Tymple, Saint Martin, Saint-Denis, Montmartre, Saint-Honoré, Saint-Jacques, rue de la Harpe, Barilleri, intersecting themselves in an incredible maze, as well as the adjacent ulcers and dead ends, were littered with a diverse mass of gory.

Louis XIII, already known to us for his uncharacteristic cleanliness for his time, tried to bring Paris to order - planted more or less significant streets with sandstone and strictly ordered them to be marked. But efforts and costs proved to be in vain. The complex mixture, which included manure, human excreta, purification of vegetables and fruits, all kinds of waste, again covered the bridges with a thick layer. It was senseless to sweep them.

Walking through the streets could come to a sorry end - passers-by could easily be soaked with the contents of a night vase or litter.

A law issued in France in 1270 prohibited the Parisians from pouring litter and sewage from the upper windows of houses to prevent the harm to people passing below. Violators were threatened by a penalty. Allegedly appeared this law after some unlucky Parisian poured litter onto the head of Louis IX!

However, there was no special benefit from this decision, and in the 14th century a new law was adopted, allowing the pouring of litter, screaming three times: "Watch out! I pour out!" The contents of the buckets and pots was spilled directly on the heads of passers-by who had to be very careful. Once you miss out, you forget to look up and then you get a nice gift right onto your head. There was no chance to escape in the middle of the street: the width of the majority of "an avenue" did not exceed 8 meters, and some were even 1-2 meters wide. In addition to pedestrians, equestrians, carriages and herds of distilled animals could be seen on them.

There were no concepts of disinfection: in addition to the usual dirt in the apartments of commoners, bourgeois and aristocrats, lice, bedbugs and fleas were soaked. The butchers, in full view of everybody, slaughtered the cattle on the streets, spreading the intestine, draining blood on the sidewalks, thus reinforcing the overall stink.

A French chronicler reported in 1400 that huge piles of garbage near the walls of Paris were equal in height to the gate. Garbage in general became a real bane of urban settlements. In the mid-14th century, it was one of the causes of the terrible bubonic plague epidemic, which, according to some estimates, destroyed half of the population of Europe. Only this made the authorities think about the sanitary condition of the cities. In France and England fines were imposed for dumping garbage on city streets (a telling example: in the archives of the English city of Stratford-on-Avon, evidence was found that William Shakespeare 's father was fined for throwing litter in the street).

In England and many German states, it was prohibited to dump debris near water sources (this did not prevent it from being dumped in swamps, which were often sources of rivers and streams). 1588 gave the first ever example of tax incentives for garbage disposal: Queen Elizabeth I of England (1533-1603) gave special tax privileges to collectors of cloth that was used for paper production.

Still the main rescue of the city was the rain. Washing the streets, it drove the flows of scum through them.

Clean water in cities has become a mythical phenomenon. The liquid that replaced it for washing and cooking purposes was so dirty that no one had arguments against the author's version of the article "Life in the 1500's," popular throughout the English-speaking Internet. He quite conclusively linked the saying about "throwing the baby out with the bathwater" to the abomination that splashed in the dirty containers used in the household.

At some point in the walled cities and fortresses there appeared built-in toilets, where, however, not everyone had access to. However, those who got there were enough to dip into the creepy malice of the outer side of the city walls and the defensive moat surrounding them.

The problems of the air environment of Paris were exacerbated by constant population growth, which led to an increase in the height of houses and the narrow streets. In most pathetic rooms, especially in heavily populated poor neighborhoods like Saint-Jacques-de-la-Boucherie or the neighborhood of Saint-Marseille, there was little light or air passing. The city authorities because of the need to build sacrificed the need for open air.

French media historian Fernan Braudel gave a merciless description of the interior of a conventional house in medieval Europe: "The floor on the ground floor will be made from packed soil for a long time, and then it will be covered with stone tiles or ceramic tiles. The ceiling has long been referred to as the "floor": it was actually just the floor of an attic or an overlying floor; outward-projecting beams supported it: untreated in row houses, shaded, decorated or tissue-inhabited - in rich dwellings. The most curious custom of the old times up to the 16th century and even later is to cover the floors of the first floor and living rooms with straw in winter and green leaves, and with flowers - in summer... The heating was bad, ventilation was ridiculous, food was cooked the rustic way.

And the night pots kept being poured into the windows, as they always have - the streets were cloaks. The bathroom was a rare luxury. Fleas, lice and bedbugs soaked in both London and Paris, both in the dwellings of the rich and in the houses of the poor. And as for the lighting of houses, candles of different varieties and oil lamps will remain until the time when there will be - and it won't happen until the beginning of the 19th century - a blue flame of lighting gas... So if we appeared in the interiors of past times as intruders, we would quickly feel misplaced out there. Their excesses, no matter how beautiful they are (and often they were amazing!), would not be enough for us."

In the absence of official janitors, the citizens themselves sometimes tried to clean the streets of Paris. The first such "subbotnik" took place in 1662, in honor of which the proud Parisians beat out a commemorative medal.

On the shores of the muddy and polluted Thames

In posh London, the sanitary condition was no better than in the French capital. A prominent representative of the Renaissance philosopher Erasm of Rotterdam (1469-1536), who had been to England on several occasions, complained in a letter to his friend: "I am struck and oppressed by the idea that for many years England has been chronically struck by plague contagion... All floors here are made of clay and covered with swamp stone, and this bedding is so rarely renewed that the lower layer often lies for at least 20 years. It is impregnated with saliva, excreta, urine of people and dogs, spilled beer, mixed with fish and other scum. When the weather changes, the floors emit such a smell, which I believe in no way can be beneficial to health."

On the streets there was such a stench that the city fathers used to hold in their hands balls of perfume pomade during the processions, and women used to hang chains with such balls on their necks or put bouquets in the cleavage, as it was thought to help from infection.

In rich Englishmen's houses, it was in fashion to pour the contents of night pots into fireplaces or simply urinate there. It must be recognized that this is a relatively acceptable method of utilization of excreta, from the point of view of hygiene although, of course, it did stink.

Commoners, who were no proud owners of fireplaces, as well as everywhere in Europe, spilled the contents of night vases from their windows. In order to save the nightwalkers from the neighbors' waste products, the Londoners hit upon the idea of creating a special night guard – "charlie." They monitored the order in general, and in particular were obliged to observe the windows. As soon as the hand with the pot was showing there, "charlie" started shouting loudly, warning the passers-by. It was a kind of sport. An idle inhabitant of the British capital is trying to slosh a passer-by (the richer the better), "charlie" is yelling, a terrified passer-by is jumping aside...

Londoners took water for cooking from wells, not from the polluted Thames, of course. However, all sorts of mud inevitably penetrated the aquifers, thus poisoning the wells.

Poor Thames! Already in the 13th century, cattle catchers and leather tunders actively worked on its banks. In 1290, the monks of one of the monasteries complained to King Henry III about the smell of the Thames, so terrible that even the rook could not overrun it. After 50 years, Newgate Street butchers were officially allowed to use a wharf near Flit Prison to ripple the insides.

What was the sewer of London like in the late Middle Ages? Predictably, its infrastructure was confined to watershoots laid downhill towards the Thames. Of course, the ditches of this kind got filled to overflowing extremely quickly, directing muddy flows into the streets, sometimes into the poorly constructed buildings.

Tired of this evil madness, King Henry VIII (1491-1547) issued a decree requiring the homeowners to clean areas of sewage canals. In addition, the King created a Runoff Commission to enforce these rules. However, the monarch did not provide funding for its work. So in fact, the Commission did not begin its work until 122 years later, when it was decided to use the fines for non-fulfilment of the decree in order to keep it working. The clerk kept daily records about the Commission's activities. The citizens sent alarming messages there.

In the early 18th century, almost every London house acquired a pit. These pits spread the horrible stench that poisoned of wealthy aristocrats' staying at home. The smell inside the houses was no better than on streets polluted with litter and excreta. People were tormented but preferred to still sit in their dwellings rather than breathe the unhealthy air of the City, full of coal smoke and sulfur factory smog, which often caused "mysterious deaths" from asphyxiation. Wealthy residents from the upper classes sprayed sheets with perfumes to deodorize their houses.

When the pits under the houses were filled, their contents were withdrawn through primitive drainage pipes into the above mentioned semi-open waste ditches laid in the middle of the street. Liquid from waste pits often eroded the foundations, walls and floors of residential buildings. Drainage pipes got clogged, with waste spilling under the house. Children who were able to penetrate the most difficult-to-reach corners were usually hired to clean the waste pits and disposal pipes. This affected children's health in the most harmful way, often resulted in deaths, and caused long-term diseases. The actual construction of the sewerage in London started only after "The Great Stink" of 1858 when, with water level rise in the Thames the inhabitants of City were forced to escape while the Parliament continued to sit behind the curtains laced with chloric lime.

Not a step without the stilt

The German lands fragmented in the Middle Ages were no better than their European neighbors in terms of sanitation were. The history of Germany knows a case truly tragic: in 1183 in Erfurt Castle, in Thuringia, the floor of the main hall broke, and the power Emperor of the Holy Roman Empire Frederick I Barbarossa (1122-1190) and his knights fell directly into sewage. The emperor survived, but many counts and barons drowned. After this occasion, many German feuds chose to rebuild their castles using a system of drain gutters draining away behind the walls into the fortress moat. What happened next to these moats and walls - you already know.

Sometimes the engineering ideas went further - in Burg Elz Castle, located near the Trier where t St. Simeon lived in his own defecation, the toilet was in the side tower. When rainwater was gathering upstairs, the shutter opened, washing away the sewage. How was the task of washing away in drought periods solved? It's anyone's guess.

The author of the book "Western Europe XI-XIII centuries" Alla Yastrebitskaya writes: "At the end of the 15th century the residents of the town of Reitling persuaded the emperor Frederick III (1440-1493) not to come to their town, however he did not listen to the advice and nearly died in dirt together with his horse..."

If you had ended up in the spring on the street of a medieval German city, surely you would have experienced a cultural shock. Including people on... stilts. Yes, the stilts that you won't see today anywhere except at the circus, at some point became part of everyday life. It was resolutely impossible to move around the dirty streets without this "spring shoes" during mud season. Stilts spread across the continent, and in some cities, even competitions on agility using stilts were held. Alternatively, socles, i.e. wood stands for women's street shoes, to which they were joined with belts - were invented in Italy.

Proof that the medieval mud of Europe had also moved to more enlightened centuries can be found in the travel essays and letters of the Russian dramatist, the author of "The Minor" Denis

Fonvizin, who at the end of the XVIII century had done a lot of crisscrossing abroad. He writes with great delight about the French theatre, Italian singing school, Prussian innovations in agriculture, museums, cathedrals and palaces of Europe. Nevertheless, there are other lines...

"In the morning we came to Rossitten to change horses. Rossitten is a most lousy village. The postmaster lives in a house so messy that we could not get into it... We arrived in Konigsberg on the 30th. Although I was never fascinated by it, it seemed gloomier to me when I arrived there now.

What I disliked most was the following custom: at eight o 'clock they usually have dinner and at eight sewage is removed from the village.

Stilts became widespread both in rural areas and in cities.
In some places, they even organized competitions -fights on

Such a custom gives a clear concept of both smell and tastes of Konigsberg residents... From my journal, you will see that the whole way from Leipzig to this city was very hard for us. The roads are hell, the food is bad, and the beds are showered with bedbugs and fleas... Bolzano is lying in a pit. The way of life is Italian, that is – there are loads of dirt. The stone floors are dirty; the linen is nasty; bread, which even beggars would not eat; their clean water is our sewage... In the morning we took the mail, we went from stingy Bolzano to Trento, which further led us into frustration. In the best public house, all you find is stink, impure, abomination..."

By the way, in France Fonvizin acquired the glory of the owner of numerous wealth, as he took a bath every day.

Europe in the centuries we are addressing is not only Paris bedbugs and excreta-filled castle walls. During this period, the European continent went from the grim reality of the early middle Ages to the rapid development of the science and arts of the Age of Enlightenment. Many of the things created in those years entered the gold pool of humankind. We will not forget that many technologies, including sanitary and hygienic technologies, were in their embryo state at that time.

The achievements of the great Asian peoples due to the lack of dialogue of cultures reached Europe much later. The legacy of ancient Rome has been forgotten largely for ideological reasons. Life was strongly invaded by religious prejudices and ridiculous myths, which had no one to refute. Therefore, we are not entitled to blame the ancestors of current Europeans – we should take pity for them instead. After all, if desired, the same collection of facts can be collected about the medieval life of almost any people, any state or region. Lack of food, low level of education and medicine, artisanal production, inability to provide the majority of the population with the most necessary things. All this gave an opportunity for commodious existence (by today's standards – relatively commodious) to those who were at the top of the social pyramid. The rest led a life truly miserable, famished and poor. Dirt, parasites, epidemics and stink were inevitable companions of such social existence.

CHAPTER IV.

What Did Baldini Trade In?

Baldini had thousands of them. His stock ranged from essences absolues-floral oils, tinctures, extracts, secretions, balms, resins, and other drugs in dry, liquid, or waxy form-through diverse pomades, pastes, powders, soaps, creams, sachets, bandolines, brilliantines, mustache waxes, wart removers, and beauty spots, all the way to bath oils, lotions, smelling salts, toilet vinegars, and countless genuine perfumes.

Patrick Süskind.

"Perfume: The story of a murderer"

We have already found that general hygiene in the middle Ages was not at the highest level. However, the highest to know at some point began to conclude that unpleasant smells should be _____ with something, smoothing their sharpness, scoring with pleasant, stronger flavors.

Perfumery and medicine

Masters of the production of primitive cosmetics and perfumes have survived, first of all, in Italian lands - heirs of ancient Rome, advanced in this respect. We should of course mention the East, where the flavors were managed in a very skillful way. Other countries were less fortunate, including France. And already in 1190 King Philip-August (1165-1223) issued incentive rules, granting privileges to those "who have the right to cook and sell powders, pomades, ointments for whiteness and cleaning skin, soap, floral waters, gloves and leather products".

The ladies of the European Middle Ages, who have long used the natural excretions of their bodies as perfume, lubricating them upon the areas of skin behind their ears and on their necks, have now received at their disposal a wider line of perfumery products.

However, the own creations of European alchemists-perfumers, unrelated to the experience of Eastern masters, at first were disgusting rather than odoriferous substances. Believing that the more contrasting the ingredients are, the more interesting is the result, they experimented by mixing the levee infusion with the thickened legs of dried toads or cooking rose petals together with horse manure...

The capital of perfume was commercial Venice. Here the spices brought from the East - pepper, nutmeg, cloves buds, cinnamon, ginger, saffron, cardamom were processed. As well as European thyme, basil, sage... The creations of perfumers were not then divided into ladies' and men's fragrance. Strong fragrances included snuff. It consisted of complex compounds of arid fragrant plants, which may not even contain tobacco leaf particles at all. Both men and women sniffed these mixtures.

In France, the use of perfume reached its height under King-Sun Louis XIV. Note that pouring himself with perfume was intended not only to save aristocratic noses, but also to strengthen the natural protective forces of the body, which were thought to catalyze aromatic essences. Unlike "malicious water". The functions of perfume and pharmaceuticals merged.

The active use of flavours is due to this belief in their hygienic and preventive properties. Ladies and men rubbed the skin with fragrant soap, rinsed with aromatic vinegar, applied sweet almond ointments to their hands, greased their hair with sandal, lavender, jasmine oil. The association of pharmaceuticals and perfumery successfully illustrates the famous in due time "Water of the Queen of Hungary." This fragrant liquid based on rosemary was endowed with simply fantastic preventive and healing qualities. Legend has it that the old queen of Hungary was cured with its help of all the infirmities, regained her beauty and the Polish king proposed to her. The 17th-century Paris surgeon, publisher of the first-ever special medical journal Nicolas de Blégny described the effect of this drug this way. If you wet the back of your head, temples and wrists, it restores evaporated bodily spirits, cleans your stagnant nerves, improves your memory, gives you good sense, strength and fun, and invigorates feelings.

Smell alone cures the headache. If you put a cotton impregnated with it in your ears, it will eliminate sputum and tinnitus. If you apply it to your stomach, it will alleviate almost all abdominal pain. If you apply it to your eyelids, it will strengthen your vision. If you wash your whole body with it, it will help against apoplexy, paralysis, gout and rheumatism. "Queen of Hungary's Water" allegedly also helped with tumors, bruises and burns.

When Louis XIV began to develop a tumor in 1686, he was treated with a fragrant patch, which included galbanum, opoponax, myrrh, frankincense and mastic, among other ingredients. Like all doctors of the time, His Majesty's court doctors believed that the vitality of these smelling favors could heal from the tumor.by penetrating inside the body,

A little later, just in the "Grenoillean" era, a sympathetic concept is becoming popular in Europe, its adherents claimed that people spread around themselves particles of an invisible substance called sympathetic. It affects our senses, causing inclination or disgust, sympathy or antipathy. Knowing the secrets of this substance, you can manage the sympathies of people, and even the love of men and women. At the same time, it was claimed that a red–haired woman radiates attraction constantly, because the strength of her smell does not depend on the life cycles of ordinary people.

Faith in the pharmacological merits of plant extracts has contributed to their spread and even technological progress. When one of Louis XIV's court doctors invented a sprayer for favors, he hastened to assure the monarch of the therapeutic significance of his invention: thanks to it, fragrant compositions will penetrate directly into the lungs, heart and blood vessels, fully preserving healing properties.

The perfumers could make a considerable fortune since the aristocrats were generous wishing to smell in accordance with fashion.

"This commonality of medicine and perfumes is also evidenced by a lot of other, not so multifunctional products", writes

Annik Le Gerer. "For example, "cuquifs", therapeutic caps packed, depending on the financial capabilities of the owner, either with favors, gum and wood resin, or musk and ambra. They are worn both at night and during the day under a hat... There are also cosmetic fabrics and handkerchief. A Venus's handkerchief is a piece of canvas soaked for many days in aromatic compositions; Dried, it is used for dry face washing. According to the same principle, night chaps and bandages are made to protect against wrinkles. In aromatic compositions, linen used for purely medical purposes is soaked. I will mention only a few such devices, where flavours are used for pinpoint preventive measures These are both "invigorating bandages" which protect the doctor's face at the head of the plague patient, and "protective shirts" specially flavored for work in the hospital and designed to protect against dangerous vapours, which come from the conceived. For the latter shrouds impregnated with odours are intended. All these means should prevent the spread of the plague spirit by "neutralizing" it with good smells. As one of Louis XIV 's doctors, Abbot Rousseau, argued: "The whole action of the medicine is to pass them a certain smell." This also applies to healing compositions comprising substances of animal or human origin with a nausea spirit. This is, for example, the "universal remedy" recommended by Abbot Rousseau. Despite the components such as testicles, kidneys and genitals of a deer, human excreta, urine and blood, this balm must have a pleasant flavor".

So here are the ideas in which the author of the horrible recipe, the above mentioned Crollius drew inspiration! After all, abbot Russo said directly, "Since man is the lord of all creatures, no animal can compare its healing properties with the human body".

However, by the time J. B. Grenouille first peeped into Baldini 's shop, the confidence in the preventive and healing efficiency of the flavours started leaving the educated public. Perfume separated from pharmaceuticals, becoming a completely independent industry. The masters of the perfume shop, gradually improving the distillation processes, started creating increasingly subtle flavours.

However, outdated perceptions of the healing potential of flavors continued for some time. Shortly before the Great French Revolution, the renowned chemist Furcroix even developed a classification of medicines based on their odors. Grey ambra, muscus, cibet and sandalwood according to this author stimulate nerves and heart. Plants with a tolerant smell such as garlic, leek, galbanum, opoponax are allegedly effective protective means against the plague.

By the way, in England the cosmetic experiments of the French and the Italian were not approved, not for medical reasons, but for ethical reasons. In the early 17th century, the British Parliament issued a law stating that women who seduced His Majesty 's subject King of England by perfumery, face paint, false teeth, high heels and this would induce men to marry would be as punished as witches and other similar criminals; Such marriages would be considered null and void.

At the Pont au Change

Describing Baldini 's shop, Patrick Süskind gives many names of exquisite flavors and cosmetics many of which are completely unknown to the general public. Could it be so that the author simply made them up? Let's take, for example, storax, a component of the perfume called "Amor and Psyche" made by social-climber Pelicier, which the elderly Baldini unsuccessfully sought for? Storax is nothing more than a resin that flows from a damaged benzoin tree growing on the Indonesian island of Sumatra. Because the storax has a very strong smell, the bottle with it was placed into an abdominale membrane of a bull in those days. Storax can be found and tasted in modern Russia: it is found in imported cookies with aromatic glaze. The coating resin is designated on the packages as a food additive E906.

And what is pure zibetum (or rather civet), "one extra drop can lead to catastrophic consequences" for the perfume producer? This is the emanation of the proctal glands of some types of civet cats, predatory animals living in Asia and Africa. Civet has an exceptionally strong musk smell and is terribly expensive even now that aromatics have learned to synthesize. In the 18th century, a small batch of civets cost a fortune. It is extracted by binding the animal to rods and squeezing out saltlike contents of glands, scraping with a spoon or collecting the same spoon from stones on animal paths.

Or another: "He kneaded in the dough some incense, shellac, vetiver and cinnamon and rolled smoking balls out of it". Cinnamon and incense are clear and obvious. Unlike shellac and vetiver. But, as it turns out, all these ingredients Süskind didn't make up. Vetiver is a herb that grows in tropical and subtropical countries. The aromatic properties of vetiver roots have been known since ancient times, and it has been used in the East as a raw material for smoking. The roots contain a yellow-red or brownish viscous oil with a strong and stable flavor of wood, earth and smoke-like nature.

From the same places comes shellac that is a red resin-like substance which is released by female insect kerria lacca to put eggs in it. Shellac ices the young twigs of the trees on which these insects live (most often these are different kinds of ficus), and after young insects hatch from the eggs, the twigs dry up. These branches 5-10 cm long are washed and processed on red paint and yellow-brown shellac resin. The possibilities of using shellac are surprising in their diversity. Lacquers, insulating materials, phonorecords, shoe polish and the like, and at the same time glazes for coating tablets and candy, are made from it.

"Andrew's grass (speedwell) had to be carefully overrun, cracked, chopped, stuffed..." In the original German source, Süskind uses the word "Andres" as the name of this plant raw material. We will consider that the translation is accurate. In such a case, there were herbs and subshrubs united in the genus Veronica. They were used mainly in folk medicine. Nevertheless, there is evidence that Andrew's grass could have been used as a perfume, apparently for this Baldini and distilled it in his cube.

The powder of wheat (or rice) flour, which Jean-Baptiste learned to mix from Baldini, had been given the rank of a cosmetics product that was almost mandatory for a woman and desirable for men by Marquise de Pompadour. Imitating the marquise, the ladies loaded on their heads giant wigs, which depicted real paintings - for example, a seascape or landscape. It took whole kilograms of powder. Therefore, the long known to humankind cereal powder went into fashion again in the 17th century. It was generously sprinkled not only onto the hairstyle, but also onto exposed body parts. The courtiers applied a thick layer of powder to their face, shoulders, hands, giving them aristocratic paleness and hiding blemishes. Color powder was also popular - gentle pink stressed the natural blush of cheeks, blue one was superimposed under the eyes. Even such exotic devices (from the point of view of our contemporaries) as powder cabinets are known. The ladies covered their dresses with a case, after which they entered the closet and took a "charge" of powder.

To ensure better retention of rice powder on the body, viscosity-enhancing substances - lead white and bismuth salts with arsenic admixture - were added to it. So much wheat and rice went to the powder that soon - after the Great French Revolution - powder production was banned in France and some other European countries. People were starving, there were more important things to think about than cosmetics.

Full rehabilitation of powder occurred only in the early 20th century: theatre actresses concealed skin blemishes with the help of makeup not only on stage, but also in real life. And then in France, powder was invented almost in its modern form, i.e. based on talc.

"...And molded fat sticks, carmine-red, for lips." Of course, it is about lipstick. They made them only from natural products, and it was used by men as well - so that the contours of the mouth were visible and did not merge with the beard and moustache.

Süskind's above mentioned "brilliant father of perfume Maurizio Francipani" never really existed. The German novelist, in order to simplify the narrative, combined in the image of one person the achievements of an entire family of perfumers belonging to the ancient Roman patrician lineage. One of them came up with "Franjipani powder" back in the 15th century. The principle of its formulation was simple and complex at the same time. All the strongest flavors known at that time, apart from the ground root of iris, musk and civet, were mixed in equal proportion. The same amount of iris was then added to this mixture, and finally in a ratio of 1:100 to musk and civet. Strong-smelling powder became widespread among the European elite. It, in particular, was used for rubbing curtains in palace chambers to repel the widespread smell of sewage. The descendant of the inventor – also a Francipani, named Mercurio, found that the aroma stays longer if the powder is spread in wine alcohol. Thus, he created the first perfume - dissolved in alcohol smelling substances.

Muzio Francipani brought this perfume to Paris. And it was his grandson, that had exorcised his birth name and became Frangipan, who managed to reach the post of a marshal under Louis XIII and introduced perfume into fashion as a means for perfume gloves.

"Rome of aromas"

Grenouille, as you will remember, having left Paris, went to Grasse, as Master Baldini called it, "Rome of flavors, the promised land of perfumers." What kind of city is it?

The most effective protection against plague in the middle Ages was considered leather gloves protecting one's palms. One of the centers of glove production of Europe was considered the city of Grasse, which is in Provence. According to fashion historians, the European fate of gloves was changed by the wife of Henry IV and regent of his son Louis XIII Maria Medici (1575-1642), who made them a popular accessory with the nobility. Gloves were now made from thin skin, and noble ladies sought to form huge collections. And since they were unable to process the skin from which gloves were made in a proper way, they made efforts to mute the unpleasant smell of the skin with various flavors. In Grasse, they invented a way to tan skin, using a mastic tree and myrtle, which painted the product green and gave it a pleasant smell.

Progress was not stopped: Grasse masters all the time improved technical equipment, and with it and ways of exhalation of fragrance. They did not limit themselves to raw materials, fragrant plants growing in the district: lavender, orange tree flowers, myrtle, mastic tree, jasmine, rose, tuberose, and cassia. Zoogenic raw materials brought in from all sides were also used.

For example, the precious already mentioned civet: crooks diluted it on the way, so experienced customers demanded to deliver civet in a sealed buffalo horn.

According to some reports, Grasse gloves received patents for the production of perfume as early as 1614 from the hands of Louis XIII. In 1656 in Grasse, there appeared the first French "Guild of Glovers-Perfumers" (gantiers-parfumeurs), who received the patent from Louis XIV. . In 1730, former gloves founded a perfumer shop in Grasse, switching exclusively to the manufacture of perfumery. The art of perfume composition was also born in the workshops of Grasse and began a triumphal march through Europe. Soon perfume shops like Baldini 's ceased to be uncommon in major European cities. However, Grasse remained the capital of perfume.

Europe did not know the secrets of distillation of Arab perfumers for a long time. Nevertheless, Grasse glovers persistently sought a way of producing essential oils. Soon they rediscovered the mystery of distillation cubes, jealously safe kept by Arab masters. The distillation method became commonly known in the perfume world. However, the most delicate flowers- such as jasmine - needed to be treated differently, more gently.

This delicate method was named "enfleurage" and had three

varieties - hot, cold and oil. In the first case, the petals were laid on a wooden frame soaked with hot fat. In the second one flowers were wrapped in canvases greased with the same animal fat, and left for some time. In the third case, a gauze stretched on the frame and impregnated with olive oil was required. Cold and hot enfleurage resulted in a product called pomade. It should have been dissolved in alcohol and vigorously shaken for 24 hours to separate fat from essential oil.

By the 19th century, Grasse had finally established itself as the world's center for the production of aromatic raw materials and perfumes. And already in the 20th century this town became the homeland of the most famous aroma in the history of mankind - Chanel No. 5. Its composition was suggested to Coco by a perfumer from Grasse, Ernest Beaux.

Today, 500 tons of rose petals, 100 tons of citrus flowers, 60 tons of jasmine grown in the vicinity of this small town (40,000 inhabitants) are processed annually at Grasse factories. Tourists will discover here the International Perfume Museum and private museums of local perfume production. By the way, in one of them under the leadership of a perfumer-professional it is possible to make perfume to one's own taste.

CHAPTER V.

What Does A Human Smell Of?

From time to time he reached in his pocket and closed his hand around the little glass flacon of his perfume. The bottle was still almost full. He had used only a drop of it for his performance in Grasse. There was enough left to enslave the whole world. If he wanted, he could be feted in Paris, not by tens of thousands, but by hundreds of thousands of people; or could walk out to Versailles and have the king kiss his feet; write the pope a perfumed letter and reveal himself as the new Messiah; be anointed in Notre-Dame as Supreme Emperor before kings and emperors, or even as God come to earth-if there was such a thing as God having Himself anointed...

Patrick Süskind.

"Perfume: The story of a murderer"

Jean-Baptiste Grenouille, in search of the perfect smell, used cold enfleurage - killing girls, wrapping bodies in fat-oiled sheets, and then extracting the aroma from fat and hair with alcohol. According to Süskind, his character managed to create the desired substance. How much does this correspond to the views of modern science?

Before we answer this question, let us look deep into our body - into the central nervous system. It turns out that smell is closer than vision or hearing is associated with brain departments, which are responsible for vegetative provision of emotions and sexual activity, and much weaker - with those areas of the brain that determine logical thinking and speech. Hence the anguish we experience trying to describe a particular smell. We can compare with another smell, but epitets to pick up... Try now to reproduce with words the smell of rose, fried potatoes or a loved one, and you will understand what it is.

Süskind conveyed this feature in a remarkable dialogue between a wet nurse Jeanne Bussie and Father Terrier.

"Aha", said Terrier with satisfaction, letting his arm swing away again. "You retract all that about the devil, do you? Good. But now be so kind as to tell me: what does a baby smell like when he smells the way you think he ought to smell? Well?"

"He smells good", said the wet nurse.

"What do you mean, 'good'?" Terrier bellowed at her. "Lots of things smell good. A bouquet of lavender smells good. Stew meat smells good. The gardens of Arabia smell good. But what does a baby smell like, is what I want to know."

The wet nurse hesitated. She knew very well how babies smell, she knew precisely-after all she had fed, tended, cradled, and kissed dozens of them... She could find them at night with her nose. Why, right at that moment she bore that baby smell clearly in her nose. But never until now had she described it in words.

"Well?" barked Terrier, clicking his fingernails impatiently.

"Well it's" the wet nurse began, "it's not all that easy to say, because... because they don't smell the same all over, although they smell good ail over, Father, you know what I mean? Their feet, for instance, they smell like a smooth, warm stone-or no, more like curds... or like butter, like fresh butter, that's it exactly. They smell like fresh butter. And their bodies smell like... like a griddle cake that's been soaked in milk. And their heads, up on top, at the back of the head, where the hair makes a cowlick, there, see where I mean, Father, there where you've got nothing left..." And she tapped the bald spot on the head of the monk, who, struck speechless for a moment by this flood of detailed inanity, had obediently bent his head down. "There, right there, is where they smell best of all. It smells like caramel, it smells so sweet, so wonderful, Father, you have no idea! Once you've smelled them there, you love them whether they're your own or somebody else's. And that's how little children have to smell-and no other way. And if they don't smell like that, if they don't have any smell at all up there, even less than cold air does, like that little bastard there, then... You can explain it however you like, Father, but I" - and she crossed her arms resolutely beneath her bosom and cast a look of disgust toward the basket at her feet as if it contained toads - " I, Jeanne Bussie, will not take that thing back!"

The memory of the nose is difficult to state in words, but extremely useful in the struggle for existence. It allows almost instantly, without a long analysis of the facts, to take advantage of the available olfactory experience, to assess the situation and to make the only right decision.

Another important aspect. Today science is dominated by the hypothesis that the attitude towards smells, the division of them into pleasant and unpleasant ones is, most likely, an inherited rather than acquired quality of man. At least it is proved by experiments with young children. As well as a fact almost unquestioned by anyone: representatives of very distant cultures with regard to odors show rare consensus. This feature of the human body - a fixed reaction to certain smells, the ability to influence the mental state with their help - is at the heart of aromatherapy. As well as some practical recommendations. For example, mint gum for increasing attention is given to soldiers of some armies of the world.

Everyone knows the importance animals attach to the smells of their relatives. Look at a dog sniffing the corner of the house - it is indeed hard work of the nose, reading multiple information about the dogs noted here earlier. What about the man?

In the cultures closest to nature, not damaged by the conditions of civilization, the smell of the body is paid special attention to. "The Australians from the Burarra tribe, seeing a friend in the off, spends his hand under his armpit and then - on the naked chest of a friend: let's say, we break up, but my spirit will remain with you. Bushmen of Kalahari perform similar actions during magical rites of treatment, aboriginal people of Papua New Guinea - in childbirth. The significance of symbolic action is obvious: the smell of a man is perceived as part of himself, and people seek to transfer a particle of themselves to those who they want to help", writes the popularizer of science E. Tichenko in the Chemistry and Life magazine.

As a result of numerous experiments it was revealed that the smell of "friend" from the smell of "foe" can be distinguished not only by a "caveman", but also an urbanized person living in the conditions of modern civilization. Most people easily identify from a pile of other clothes those worn by relatives. The smell of a sexual partner, your child or your mother seems more pleasant than the smell of strangers.

But in order to become native and loved not only for a close person, but also for completely unfamiliar citizens - for this it is necessary to find a real formula of love, a formula which with dis-empowered cruelty was made by the hero of Süskind's novel.

For the first time, a group of Nobel laureates lead by the great German biologist Adolf Butenandt isolated substances having an insurmountingly attracting effect on the opposite sex, in the late 1950s. Outstanding scientific achievement was preceded by truly titanic work. In order to obtain several grams of this sub-stance - an attractant - it was necessary to "recycle" several hundred thousand unfertilized female bombyxes. (silk moth)

Mammals followed the insects, and all of them in the course of experiments surrendered to the will of the winner - concentrated aroma of attractants. Soon they learned to make artificial - synthetic - attractants for animals. However, all this, understand-ably, was only a prelude to performing a truly blood-stirring task - creating a universal flavor of love for humans.

Humans do not possess glands that release musk - a smelling sebaceous secret that attracts individuals of the opposite sex, - unlike beavers or crocodiles. However, there are apocrine sweat glands (in the area of axillary cavities, as well as in the lower part of the abdomen, on the pubic and on the genital organs). They de-velop by the time of puberty, function during one's whole life and physiologically fade only with the onset of senile shredding. It is there, according to some physiologists, that human attractants are concentrated - derivatives of testosterone hormone - closely related androstenone and androstadienone, as well as androstenol. They, as chemists found out, were imitated in many of the most valuable components of perfume, popular for many centuries – in musk produced by musk deer or civet. And, it can also be found in plant aphrodisiacs - truffles and celery!

Androstenone and androstadienone provoke discussions among specialists. The fact is that these substances cause different reactions - it depends on who inhales them. To some people smell seems pleasant, like floral or vanilla. To someone, it is unpleasant, like the smell of sweat or urine. In addition, some people do not feel it at all! *we don't react the same to odors*

Recently, neuroscientists at Rockefeller University (New York City) disseminated the results of their studies showing that differences in the perception of the odors of these substances are related to genetic differences in humans. Inhalation of androstenone and androstadienone causes a physiological response in many - but not all - men and women. Whether this is sufficient basis to recognize these substances as an unconditional attractant is the subject of scientific discussion. Curiously, at the same time androstenone is a generally recognized attractant...of pigs. In the body of boars, it is contained in saliva and urine, and its perception causes in females "effect of immobility": hearing the smell, they bend their back, taking a pose as convenient as possible for copulation.

Experiments with these substances gave a lot of food for thought. For example, the chair in the doctor's reception, "inflated" with androstenone, attracted women. They chose it among others with an error-eliminating frequency. Nevertheless, men, on the contrary, infiltrated the inflated chair with hatred and bypassed it.

Another - purely female - drug scientists found in the most

obviously adapted place of the female organism. Although experiments with volatile acids isolated from the vaginal secretory products (remember the beauty of the Middle Ages, which without any advice from the biologists used their own excretions as perfume?), gave mixed results. In some cases the sexual attractiveness of ladies covered in perfume containing these acids increased markedly, in other cases everything remained unchanged. At the same time, it was found that these acids are not synthesized in all women's organisms.

Scientists of the University of California, who set an experiment on 48 women, obtained optimistic results for perfumers. Half were offered 20 breaths of vapours of a substance containing androstenedione, a steroid hormone produced by both male and female organisms. The mixture was provided to test women in the flask and had a vivid musky smell. The rest of the tested women inhaled the substance containing yeast as many times as the first group. Two hours after the end of the trial, saliva samples were taken from all women from which scientists determined the endocrine profile of the body. Women who inhaled androstenedione reported a marked improvement in mood and an increase in libido, which was not observed in the control group.

Lots and lots of experiments had been carried out. But never - never! - in laboratories there was anything similar to the ecstatic group orgy in Grasse described by Süskind. It seems that man is still a much more complex creature than other mammals, not only because of his mindfulness. We do not simply fall for the smell. Another reason is that men and women have a more elaborate endocrine profile than males and females of other mammals. Speaking of them, the inducing chemicals of males are not formed in females' organisms and vice versa. Whereas androstenone and androstenol stand out with both men and women. The difference is in the proportion: women have higher relative content of androstenol, but the total amount of both steroids is bigger in men.

In addition, the clearance in solving the great task of discovery is universal Flavor of Love, one for men and women, similar to that created by the hero of Patrick Süskind's novel is hardly visible. Apparently, this task will remain unresolved. Well, good for us! Just imagine a world in which the mentioned perfume has spread. It will go crazy!

AND FINALLY...

Grimal 's tannery in which little Grenouille used to work, could not be located in the Paris street rue de la Mortellerie (now known as rue de l'Hôtel-de-Ville). The thing is, it is located in downtown. Back in 1702, long before Grenouille was born, the Sun King moved the leather men beyond the borders of the French capital so that they would not drain their evil waters into the Seine in the city line. The tanners moved to the suburb of Saint-Marseille, on the Bièvre River, which flows into the Seine upstream of the capital.

***

The theory of lethal fluid, which was defended by the novel character marquis de La Taillade-Espinasse, is purely parodical and completely invented by Süskind. Paracelsus's follower, eso-terist A. Mesmer, introduced the term fluid, meaning human-gen-erated magnetic energy.

***

Anthrax, which Grenouille had been down with while working in Grimal 's tanning, is indeed a "terrible disease of tanners." Süskind did not exaggerate it at all. The source of this dangerous disease is usually herbivorous domestic animals and, above all, cattle. And after the death of the infected animal, its skin remains contagious for a long time. A person can catch any infection easily when freshening and cutting carcasses, working with skin. There-fore, anthrax can be called a professional disease of those who oc-cupationally communicate a lot with animals, including tanners.

***

Baldini 's shop and house could well be located right on the bridge over the Paris River Seine - the Pont au Change. For us it is unusual and strange - a bridge that has buildings on its surface . Don't be surprised. In the times mentioned in the book, such crossings through water arteries in cities were built up quite densely. The Pont au Change, however, stood out of the crowd. It had the glory of little more than the financial center of Paris. And, of course, the concentration of a variety of shops designed for a demanding audience – "fashion boutiques" of that times. However, despite such a reputation, the Pont au Change suffered from constant destruction, as did other medieval bridges.

The stone Pont au Change was built in 1639-1647. Its building consisted of two rows of identical houses divided by a rather broad road.

On the first floors, there were shops of rich managers and shops, above them there were kitchens, even higher - three residential floors and an attic.

The poet Claude Le Petit, a hundred years before the events described in the book, wrote:

Et si par un malheur estrange,
On te ravaude tous les jours,

On t'a bien nommé Pont au Change,
Parce que tu change tousjours.

(And if by a strange misfortune,
You are mended every day,
You were named well the Pont au Change
Because you keep changing all the time.)

All the buildings from the Pont au Change were demolished at the end of the 18th century...

REFERENCE

Le Guerer A. Les parfumus a Versailles aux XVII et XVIII siecles: approche epistemologique // Odeurs et parfums / Textes rassembles et publies par D. Musset et Cl. Fabre-Vassas. P.: Ed. du CTHS, 1999.

Braudel F. Civilisation matérielle, économie et capitalisme, XVe-XVIIIe siècle. vol. 1: Les structures du quotidien - Paris: Armand Colin. 1979.

Kletschenko E. Perfume-2. Or: in the footsteps of Jean Baptiste Grenouille // Chemistry and Life, №2 – 1997.

Magne É. La vie quotidienne au temps de Louis XIII. – Hachette, Paris. - 1942.

Moulin L. La Vie quotidienne des religieux au Moyen Âge Xe-XVe siècle. - Hachette, 1990.

Neumyvakin I.P. Salajeet. Myths and Reality. - M. - SPb: Dila, 2005.

Nuremberg trial: Collection of Materials. – Moscow, Juridicheskaya Literatura, 1955.

Pognon E. La vie quotidienne en l'an mille . - Hachette littérature générale, 1981.

Russell B. A History of Western Philosophy, Simon & Schuster, Inc., 1972.

Saint-Simon A. Louis de Rouvroy. Mémoires de Saint-Simon.- Hachette et cie, 1879, №19.

Fuchs E. Illustrierte Sittengeschichte vom Mittelalter bis zur Gegenwart, Band 1: Renaissance. München: Albert Langen, 1909.

Fuchs E. Illustrierte Sittengeschichte vom Mittelalter bis zur Gegenwart, Band 2: Die galante Zeit. München: Albert Langen, 1911.

Erlanger F. Les Idées et les Mœurs au temps des rois, Paris, Flammarion, 1970.

Yastrebitskaya A. L. Western Europe of the XI-XIII centuries. - M.: Iskusstvo, 1978.

CONTENTS

Author's note.

Chapter I.

Did Jean-Baptiste Grenouille have a real prototype?

Mummies and "fresh meat"

Maniac experimenters

Chapter II

Did they really stink so badly?

Kings and bast wisp

And yet they did wash themselves!

The truth is in the middle

Lice-ridden religious teachers

Chapter III.

Is it true that cities were drowning in mud?

Are you longing to go to Paris?

Not a step without the stilt

Chapter IV.

What did Baldini trade in?

Perfumery and medicine

At the Pont au Change

"Rome of aromas"

Chapter V.

What does a human smell of?

And finally ...

References

Borzenko, Semyon Borisovich.

B82   The Code of Patrick Süskind's Perfume
Truth and fiction in the text of the famous novel

Age restrictions: 18+

Design and page proof by Polina Kirushova

Translated from Russian by Anna Silina

The publishing house requests that feedback be sent at: zistoriya-@inbox.ru

Made in the USA
Coppell, TX
25 July 2023

19570601R00042